IMAGES
of America

MILWAUKEE MAFIA

IMAGES
of America

MILWAUKEE MAFIA

Gavin Schmitt

ARCADIA
PUBLISHING

Published by Arcadia Publishing
Charleston, South Carolina

Printed in the United States of America

Library of Congress Control Number: 2012941026

For all general information, please contact Arcadia Publishing:
Telephone 843-853-2070
Fax 843-853-0044
E-mail sales@arcadiapublishing.com
For customer service and orders:
Toll-Free 1-888-313-2665

Visit us on the Internet at www.arcadiapublishing.com

To my nephew Charlie

CONTENTS

FOREWORD

Like many Milwaukeeans of Sicilian lineage, the stories of family and friends typically begin somewhere on the city's lower east side. My grandparents owned a home just blocks away from North Farwell Avenue and East Brady Street. While visiting, I vividly recall the property lines being so close one could easily eavesdrop on the quarrels of those next door. Some of these arguments (others jokingly referred to them as "intense discussions") were conducted in Sicilian, which my grandmother once described as a dialect comprised of Italian and, to a lesser extent, Arabic. Some of the stories had a seedier side, as a number of families witnessed one of their sons or grandsons go astray, tempted by the allure of the excitement and the easy money associated with the La Cosa Nostra lifestyle.

My father and mother chose to own a home on Milwaukee's west side. Even though our family lived just 10 miles west of the "old neighborhood," in reality we were worlds away from the Shorecrest Hotel on North Prospect Avenue, where Frank Balistrieri, the most influential figure in the history of Milwaukee mob, held court at Snug's Restaurant.

As a teenager, I believed that the Milwaukee mafia was part myth and part reality. Law-and-order Milwaukee police chief Harold Breier once proclaimed, "There is no prosecutable evidence of organized crime activity in Milwaukee." During the same period of time, however, two Milwaukee mobsters met their maker. On September 11, 1975, August Maniaci, an alleged gambling racketeer, was gunned down outside his Milwaukee home. Less than three years later, a suspected informer, August Palmisano, was killed when the car he started exploded.

In the aftermath of the Palmisano homicide, I began my career with the Milwaukee Police Department (MPD), sometimes patrolling the haunts of those who paid tribute to Frank Balistrieri at the Shorecrest Hotel. At the time, besides Snug's Restaurant, those assigned to the MPD's Criminal Intelligence Division (CID) believed Milwaukee's mob scene revolved around two other establishments: Sally's Steak House, owned and operated by Sally Papia, and Giovanni's Restaurant, owned and operated by Giovanni and Rosa Safina, who, sources claimed, had connections to the Chicago Outfit.

Giovanni's was one of the few establishments longtime Milwaukee County district attorney E. Michael McCann prohibited his employees from patronizing. While some in the district attorney's office privately grumbled, their boss's ban proved prudent. On March 18, 1989, an out-of-town couple in search of a hot breakfast observed a cleaning woman, bleeding from the neck, fleeing Giovanni's. Inside, police discovered Max Adonnis dead from a gunshot wound to the head. Born Maxmillan Ludwig Gajewski, the one-armed mobster worked as the restaurant's maitre d' but was purportedly involved in fencing and narcotics rackets. With the federal convictions of Frank Balistrieri and the death of Adonnis, the Milwaukee mob seemed to slip away, quietly like a ship into the night.

Some years passed before the goings-on of yore caught my attention as a supervisor of the MPD's Criminal Investigation Bureau. In 1999, a detective from the newly created MPD's Intelligence

Division located Paul Waterman, a man who stabbed and almost killed Max Adonnis on a sunny April day in 1985. When Waterman was a child, his brother apparently dabbled in the drug trade and owed Max Adonnis money. One afternoon, Adonnis, armed with a large revolver, barged into the Waterman residence located in Milwaukee's McGovern Park neighborhood and put a gun to young Paul's head. The one-armed mobster demanded to know his brother's whereabouts but left empty handed. The stress of the event, however, caused Paul Waterman to experience life-altering seizures.

Twelve years later, after Paul's father dropped him off for a visit with his Italian side of the family on Milwaukee's lower east side, Waterman caught a glimpse of the Adonnis walking near Giovanni's Restaurant. "Hey, you fat bastard!" Waterman yelled as he stabbed the mobster twice. As Adonnis clung to life, the police soon apprehended the perpetrator. At the county jail, Frank Balistrieri, who considered Adonnis a rival, dispatched his renowned defense attorney to check on Waterman. Adonnis was so despised by the district attorney's office that Waterman was given a sentence of time served and mental health treatment.

Without a doubt, the colorful lifestyles of mobsters intrigue members of the public, as many of us live vicariously through society's outlaws. As time passes, the likes of Vito Guardalabene, Joseph Vallone, Giovanni "John" Alioto, Frank Balistrieri, and Max Adonnis fade with time, which is why this book, *Milwaukee Mafia*, paints an important historical portrait of Milwaukee's past. Certainly, the vast majority of Milwaukee's Italian community is comprised of those who abide by the law, but stories persist of weddings where Italian American law-enforcement officers occupy one side of the reception hall and mobsters the other. These memories, along with the photographs of the past, serve as essential reminders of our history and heritage.

—Steve Spingola
Former Detective, Milwaukee Police Department

ACKNOWLEDGMENTS

Could Dr. Frankenstein have created his monster without Fritz? No. Could Dracula have invaded London without Renfield? No. Likewise, although I may be the author, this book could not have been assembled without many people who also deserve recognition.

Thank-you to Arcadia Publishing for giving me this opportunity and Winnie Rodgers Timmons, my editor, for believing in the project when it might otherwise have been confined to the dustbin of half-baked ideas.

Thank-you to those who helped me find these images: Harry Miller and Jennifer Graham at the Wisconsin Historical Society, Steve and Amanda at the Milwaukee County Historical Society, officer Laura Kraemer at the Milwaukee Police Department, officer Dan Buntrock of the Mequon Police Department, and Jake Ersland of the National Archives at Kansas City.

Thank-you to Det. Steve Spingola, who shared his personal files and images and wrote a glorious foreword I hope I can live up to.

Thank-you to those who helped cover the unforeseen expenses, especially Ruth Nelson, Eric Wulterkens, and Brian Q. Kelley.

Thank-you to those who provided guidance in research directions I had not previously considered: Dr. David Critchley, Tom Hunt, Rick Warner, "Rockford Mike," and especially Lennert 't Riet.

Thank-you to those who encouraged and believed in me. Too many people fit in this category to list here, but above all I must single out my best friend, Chelsea Zareczny, and my better half, Amanda Keitel.

Lastly, to anyone who reads these pages: whether your copy is purchased, borrowed, or stolen, it is your interest that made everything possible.

INTRODUCTION

Students of organized crime have seen countless books on the subject of the American mafia. New York's Five Families have been covered again and again, and the Chicago Outfit has had its share of stories told over the past century. Al Capone, all by himself, has enough biographies to fill a small library. Even relatively minor cities like St. Louis, Kansas City, Detroit, and Cleveland have had a book or two, some of them printed by Arcadia Publishing. Yet Milwaukee has never had a single book published about its criminal underworld—not one.

Sure, Jerry Capeci devotes half of a page to Milwaukee in his *Complete Idiot's Guide to the Mafia*, and Carl Sifakis gives Frank Balistrieri about the same amount of print in his *Mafia Encyclopedia*. Joseph Pistone's undercover work crippled the Milwaukee crime family, but it is hardly a focal point in his autobiography *Donnie Brasco: My Undercover Life in the Mafia*. The movie version, starring Johnny Depp, never mentions Milwaukee at all. The film *Casino* has Frank Rosenthal getting caught in a car-bomb explosion. Balistrieri, a suspect in real life, was not portrayed in the film. Milwaukee has been shortchanged again and again.

I hope the reader finds this book informative and entertaining, and I am proud that these stories are starting to be told. Throughout the course of this project, dozens of people contacted me with anecdotes of their grandmother serving FBI surveillance teams lemonade or their great-uncle's bootlegging tricks. Some were just happy to say that their parents attended high school with the children of known mafia bosses. Whether this is a history that we should embrace or discount, it is a history that demands to be examined.

As this book is largely pictorial, not all the stories can be told here. How does one portray tax evasion with a photograph? And, in many cases, images just could not be found. Milwaukee hoodlums John Triliegi and Frank Sorrenti traveled to Reno, Nevada, in 1952 and took part in the largest heist in American history. It is a fascinating story, but without pictures of Triliegi or Sorrenti it is not one that can be told in these pages.

Likewise, Milwaukee's bloodiest years will see very little coverage here. From 1910 to 1920, the rate of murders in the Third Ward broke records it had never seen before and will never see again. People would be shocked by the details surrounding the deaths of Gaetano Canizzo, Dominic Leone, Luigi Ragnetti, Albert Scorsone, Dominic Ciliberto, Michele Perricone, Carmelo Sciano, Gennaro, and Silomena Ronzio, as well as many others. The list is cumbersome.

Despite all of the omissions, readers will still find plenty to pique their interest with this book, as I have scoured the archives of police departments and prisons and found dozens of shots that have not been seen in over 50 years. Within these pages is a mug shot of Sam Vermiglio, possibly the most colorful gangster in American history. His story is unsung, but he is every bit as interesting as the names Capone or Bonanno. Also included in this book are various selections from the investigative files surrounding the murders of nightclub owner Isadore Pogrob, John DiTrapani, Frank Aiello, Albert Speciale, and Anthony Scaffidi.

In some cases, when historical photographs of buildings could not be found, modern-day images have taken their place. Readers may have been to the bookstore on Downer Avenue 50 times and never have known it had a mafia history, or perhaps a favorite tavern was once the site of a vicious shoot-out. I have opted to not provide exact addresses out of respect for the current owners, but those in the know will be able to find the hot spots easily enough.

In short, Milwaukee has experienced everything New York and Chicago has, such as counterfeiting, bootlegging, murder, hijacking, fraud, labor racketeering, and casino skimming; however, until now, the stories hardly saw print. I am honored to be the one to help change that and hope readers will begin telling stories of their own. I, for one, am all ears.

One

THE ORIGINS OF THE MILWAUKEE CRIME FAMILY

The origin of the Milwaukee mafia remains a mystery today, due chiefly to the fact that it has not been explored as thoroughly as Chicago or New York's crime families. What is known is that the first boss was Vito Guardalabene, a banker known as the "King of Little Italy" in the early 1900s.

Since the Milwaukee members were not related to the New York or Chicago members, its origins have two possibilities: the mafia sprung up independently in Milwaukee around the same time as it had in other cities, or those who formed the leadership in Milwaukee were already involved in criminal activities while living in Sicily. The former seems unlikely; the latter, while not proven, does have some evidence to support it, as the Milwaukee immigrants all came from the same region of Sicily, around the city of Bagheria.

Identifying early Milwaukee members is also not easy. Alongside the mafia, the Black Hand and the Galleani anarchists also existed. The mafia was engaged in such activities as counterfeiting, and letters from prisoners to Guardalabene show that connection. The Black Hand used threats in the mail to extort money. Some of them may have been affiliated with the mafia. In all likelihood, those who claimed to be in the Black Hand probably did not even know who else were said to be involved.

The anarchists caught many of the headlines in the early years, especially after a bomb went off at the police station, killing the most police officers in one event ever and holding that infamous distinction up through 9/11. However, with the possible exception of one man, August Chiaverotti, there was no overlap between the Italian anarchists and those in the mob.

While not all of history's mysteries have been solved, exploring them is half the fun.

Mafia members came to America from all across Sicily, settling in every major town. Interestingly, Milwaukee's crime family seems to have come entirely from the area in and around Bagheria (including Santa Flavia and Porticello). This suggests the Milwaukee members knew each other in Sicily. (Thomas Hunt.)

Santo Marino, an early member of the Milwaukee crime syndicate, was arrested with Angelo Brondo in 1909 for passing counterfeit silver certificates. After serving only one year, he remained in the mob until his death several decades later. (National Archives at Kansas City, Missouri.)

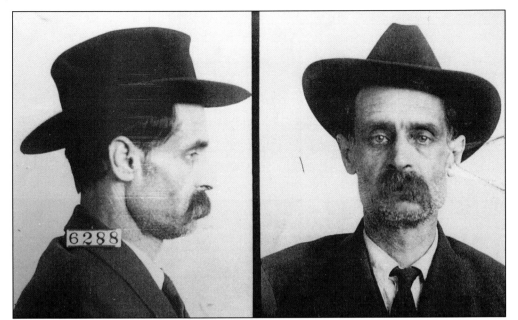

Carlos Zarcone was another counterfeiter associated with the Milwaukee underworld. Mafia historian Thomas Hunt believes that Zarcone was a distant cousin of Joseph Profaci, the founder of one of New York's Five Families. (National Archives at Kansas City, Missouri.)

Hugo Musa was the head of a counterfeiting ring that passed gold-colored lead coins around the Polish district just before Christmas in 1911. He kept police and the Secret Service busy, changing his address 25 times in three months. (National Archives at Kansas City, Missouri.)

Paul Musa assisted his older brother and had a few tricks of his own for the police. When first arrested, he falsely identified himself as Edward Simon. The next time he was collared, he was John Miller. The ruse failed when his father personally identified him. (National Archives at Kansas City, Missouri.)

The death of Vito Guardalabene in 1921 created a power vacuum in the Third Ward. Various factions fought each other for control, and there was no peace until Michele "Mike" Vitucci stepped in as the new king of Little Italy. (Author's collection.)

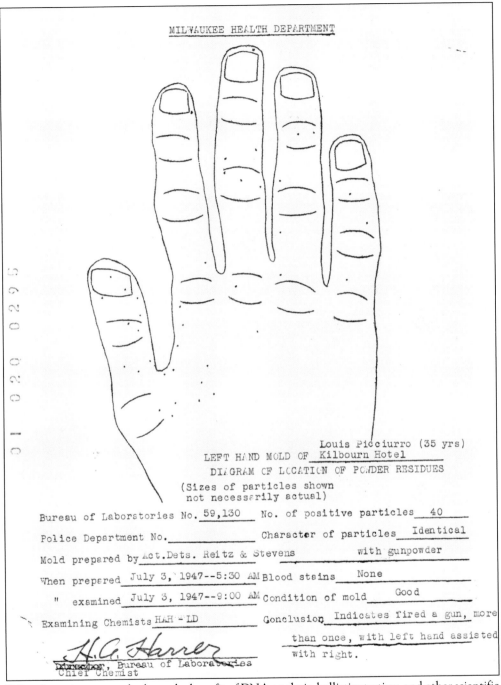

01 020 0295

Louis Picciurro (35 yrs)
LEFT HAND MOLD OF Kilbourn Hotel
DIAGRAM OF LOCATION OF POWDER RESIDUES
(Sizes of particles shown
not necessarily actual)

Bureau of Laboratories No. 59,130   No. of positive particles 40

Police Department No._____   Character of particles Identical

Mold prepared by Act.Dets. Reitz & Stevens   with gunpowder

When prepared July 3, 1947--5:30 AM Blood stains None

" examined July 3, 1947--9:00 AM Condition of mold Good

Examining Chemists HAR - LD   Conclusion Indicates fired a gun, more

                                   than once, with left hand assisted

                                   with right.

H. C. Harrer

Director, Bureau of Laboratories
Chief Chemist

Police forensic teams today have the benefit of DNA analysis, ballistics testing, and other scientific advancements. Shown here is an older method of evidence collection: a wax mold of a suspect's hand that would pick up powder particles and determine whether a gun had recently been fired. This drawing shows a hand that did indeed fire a pistol. (Milwaukee Police Department.)

Giovanni "John" Alioto, shown here in a faded FBI photograph, worked for the city as a foreman of garbage collection. Many Italian immigrants, both mob members and civilians, got their start on a garbage route. Another notable mob man in the business was Harry DeAngelo, who lied about his address to land a city job. (Federal Bureau of Investigation.)

Ernest Angelini was the first member of the Black Hand in Milwaukee to be convicted. He sent a threat through the mail to his landlord, which was quickly found to have originated with Angelini. His connection to other underworld figures is unclear. (National Archives at Kansas City, Missouri.)

Mariano "Mario" Alioto, a relative of mob boss John Alioto, was gunned down in 1917 by the Black Hand (also known as the LaFata gang) on Columbus Avenue in San Francisco while trying to fight the extortion racket. His father-in-law was killed by the same gang. (Author's collection.)

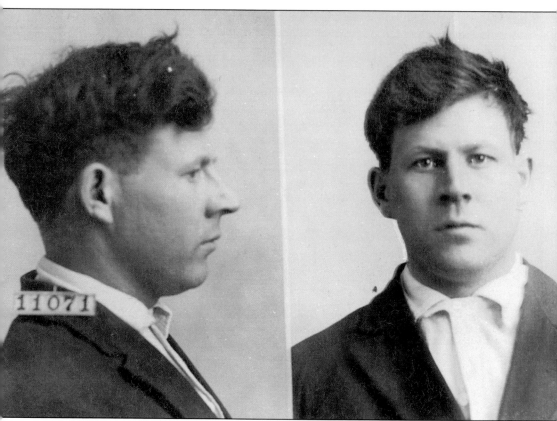

Joseph Martino tried to pass counterfeit coins in 1916. Due to his youth, one might assume that he was just a patsy or perhaps did not even know the coins were counterfeit. Martino had no known criminal record after this point. (National Archives at Kansas City, Missouri.)

Gustafetta Spera was quite the opposite of Joseph Martino. He had been personally operating a counterfeiting machine for over two years, using plaster of paris molds. His dollar coins were said to be almost perfect replicas. (National Archives at Kansas City, Missouri.)

Mayor Edward Parsons Smith identified gangster Nick Fucarino as the man who struck him over the head with a gun on September 28, 1919, during a race riot. Fucarino was held on $10,000 bond and was, in fact, able to pay. (Douglas County Historical Society.)

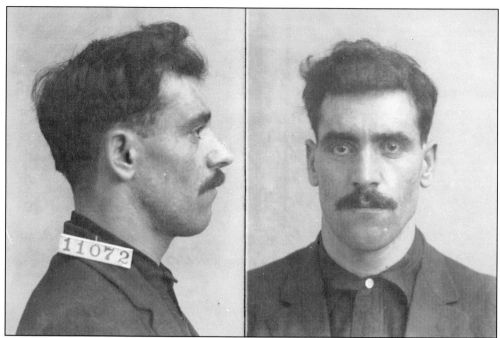

John Russo was arrested at age 25 for altering coins to make them appear more valuable than they were. This, in effect, is counterfeiting, and Russo was charged as such. Unfortunately, it does not seem that he learned his lesson in Leavenworth. (National Archives at Kansas City, Missouri.)

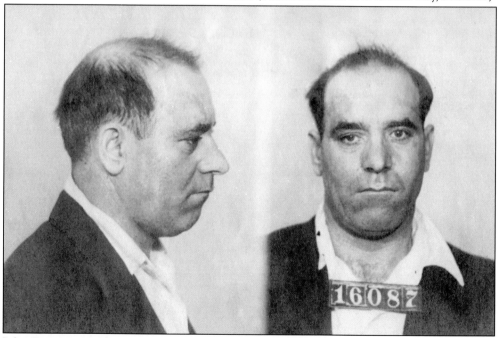

John Russo, now closer to 45 years old, was caught printing 1,000 phony Works Progress Administration (WPA) checks in Santo Maida's Chicago print shop. Thirteen other men were also rounded up by the Secret Service, including WPA employee Paul Masiolotti. (National Archives at Kansas City, Missouri.)

This building on North Broadway housed the Migliaccio & Vallone grocery. Both Joseph Vallone and Pasquale Migliaccio were high-ranking mob members, and the store was also the first place of employment for Nick Fucarino upon arriving in Milwaukee. (Milwaukee Public Library.)

Joseph Zappaterano was sent to Leavenworth on a "white slavery" charge. His family connections included the Aliotos, Gaglianos, Mancusos, and Seiditas. No direct evidence of his mafia involvement is known to exist, but he ran in the same circles, which cannot help but raise eyebrows. (National Archives at Kansas City, Missouri.)

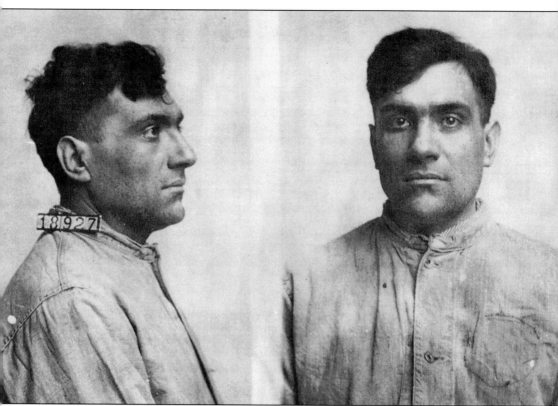

Philip Maltese was a close associate of Chicago gangster Angelo Genna. Maltese has the notorious distinction in Milwaukee history of bringing 15-year-old Genevieve Court to town and keeping her locked in a boardinghouse so that she could not testify against Maltese and Genna for forcing her into a life of prostitution. (National Archives at Kansas City, Missouri.)

Two

BOOTLEGGING AND PROHIBITION

Everybody knows that Prohibition gave rise to bootlegging, and many people are aware that bootlegging filled the wallets and bank accounts of some very unsavory men. The situation in Milwaukee was no exception.

What made the Italian-populated Third Ward the ideal place for bootlegging was that Italians already had stills in their homes. Both before and after Prohibition, it was part of the Italian tradition to make alcohol, particularly wine. This law hardly changed something that the people had done for generations out of habit. For the most part, things continued to run smoothly for the Third Ward throughout the dry years, as a jug of "Dago red," as wine was derogatorily called, could easily convince a constable to look the other way.

In his memoir *Peter's Story: Growing Up in Milwaukee's Third Ward during the 1920s and 1930s*, Peter Pizzino recalls working for the mafia as a rumrunner, making trips as far from Milwaukee as Indiana and Thunder Bay, Canada. The trade of illicit booze was not merely a local, homegrown practice; to the business savvy, it was a multistate enterprise that generated record profits and ignited an "alky war" in many cities. More Italian immigrants than can be listed here died on the streets of Milwaukee, as well as in Madison, Racine, and Kenosha, for muscling in on bootlegging territory claimed by more powerful forces.

The Chicago tentacles of Al Capone were felt in Wisconsin, as were those of his rival, Joe Aiello. One murder in Milwaukee was that of Frank Aiello, described by his friends and family as an upstanding, hard-working man with no connections to crime. A little digging by police uncovered quite the opposite.

Frank Aiello was related to Chicago's Aiello (head of the Sicilian mob), as well as numerous underworld figures in Milwaukee. The story of his death is a long one, traced to its rotten roots.

This building on Vliet Street housed Joe Pessin's elaborate bootlegging operation. Not content with merely making booze, Pessin also counterfeited labels and blew glass to make whiskey bottles appear like top-shelf brands that were available before Prohibition. (Author's collection.)

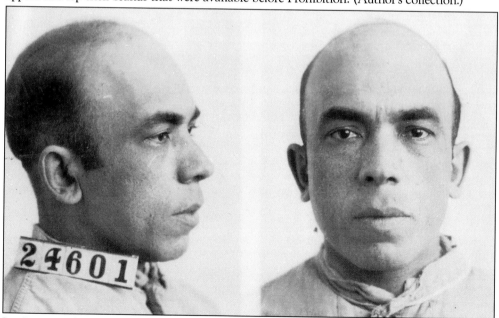

Joe Pessin is shown here after "using the mail to defraud." It was one of many arrests, most of which were for bootlegging. Despite repeated raids, Pessin simply moved his operation to another building, usually on Vliet Street. (National Archives at Kansas City, Missouri.)

Fr. Dominic Leone was a cousin to a murder victim of the same name, sanitation worker Dominic Leone. After word got out that the priest was talking to police, he was run out of town by the criminal element of Milwaukee. The murder remains unsolved. (Milwaukee County Historical Society.)

Judge John Sbarbaro's undertaking parlor on Wells Street was bombed in 1928, with one suspect being Joseph Caminiti. Sbarbaro had the distinction of not only being a judge but also a bootlegger and the man who helped bury notable gangsters Dean O'Banion, Vincent "Schemer" Drucci, Hymie Weiss, and Mike Merlo. (Author's collection.)

Shown here is the inside of the Migliaccio & Vallone store with its owners looking somewhat relaxed. Pictured from left to right are Tom Migliaccio, Pasquale Migliaccio, Jenny ? , and Joseph Vallone. Vallone was the boss of the Milwaukee crime family from 1927 through 1949, a reign second only to that of Frank Balistrieri as the longest in tenure. (Milwaukee County Historical Society.)

Vitucci's tavern comes up many times in the history of the Milwaukee underworld. Owned by Michele Vitucci and operated by Frank Vitucci, it was a favorite hangout of Det. Louis Dieden. It was also raided for bootlegging and the scene of some gunplay. (Milwaukee County Historical Society.)

William "Red" Covelli was one of Kenosha's wealthier Italians, allegedly due in part to his extensive criminal links. Police started paying more attention in 1928 when Frank Paparas was killed in Covelli's home. In later years, two of his sons would be attached the mafia. (Author's collection.)

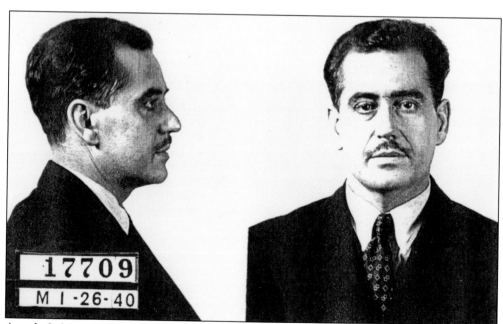

Angelo LaMantia, Frank Aiello's brother-in-law, was ultimately arrested for Aiello's murder. LaMantia was also accused of a murder in Pennsylvania and another in Sicily. By the time police caught him, key witnesses had died, and the government dropped all charges. (Milwaukee Police Department.)

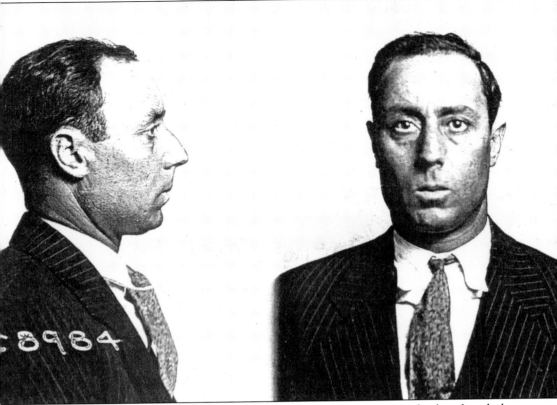

This man, Mike Bizarro, was arrested in Chicago with Angelo LaMantia, and police thought he might have answers to the Frank Aiello slaying. He did not talk and would not even identify himself, and the police were forced to release him without charges. (Milwaukee Police Department.)

Joe Stassi (pictured) was a bootlegger operating between Rockford and Racine, along with many other important figures of his day. The Stassi family also had roots in Madison; boardinghouse keeper Andrew Stassi was murdered there in May 1912 by Nicolo Quartuccio, who served 25 years in prison. (National Archives at Kansas City, Missouri.)

John Alioto's first venture into the grocery business was a small store on Van Buren Street. It was in the heart of the Italian district, which also included nearby Jackson and Jefferson Streets. The Italian neighborhoods were so tight that it was rare for anyone to remain anonymous. (Milwaukee County Historical Society.)

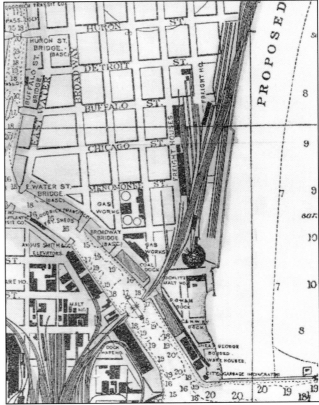

The Maniaci family was well connected in the criminal underworld. Shown here are Nunzio Maniaci (far right) and his 10 sons. Three of them—August, Vincent and Joseph—got mixed up in the mafia, and the family had blood ties to both the Rockford and Detroit mobs. (Milwaukee County Historical Society.)

The earlier years of the Milwaukee Italians (and the mafia) were spent here in the city's Third Ward. Having burned down in 1893, the immigrants had to build from scratch, cobbling together rudimentary shanties and boardinghouses. (Joshua R. Henze.)

Louis Maniaci was a cousin to the better-connected Maniaci brothers, but he was no less of a hoodlum. A brother-in-law to influential gangster Nick Fucarino, he was arrested with crews of known burglars and gamblers. (Wisconsin Historical Society.)

Frank Cosentino was found shot to
death at 40 years old in the yard of
his Twin Lakes riding stables on July
8, 1941. Police initially suspected
that a woman whose arm was
broken by Cosentino on May 8 in a
Milwaukee nightclub may have been
involved, but this theory was quickly
dismissed. (Author's collection.)

The Landgraf Hotel in Menasha was
one of several hotels around the state
that served as brothels. Prostitutes were
supplied by Milwaukee gangsters Louis
Fazio, Vincent Crupi, and attorney
Mario Megna. (Menasha Public Library.)

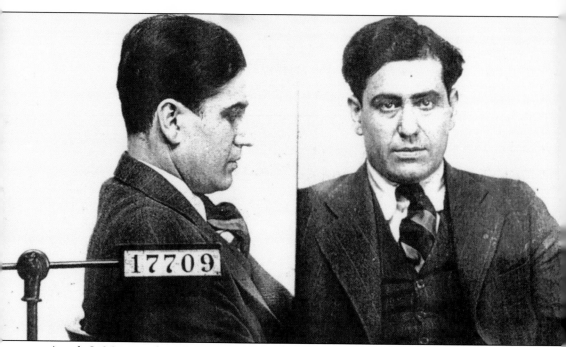

Angelo LaMantia, whose appearance varied greatly in the images depicting him, was deported to Italy to stand trial for a murder he had allegedly committed there in the 1920s. That charge was dropped, and he was extradited back to the United States for other murder trials. (Milwaukee Police Department.)

Three

PROSTITUTION

If the mafia's income sources had to be summed up in three words, they would be bootlegging, gambling, and prostitution.

Prostitution in Milwaukee today is largely unorganized, ranging from classy call girls to women working the street or in thinly veiled massage parlors. At one time, things were different. In the 1920s, vice lord Vincent Crupi operated brothels throughout the city and provided girls for many more cities throughout the state. When he was deported, this did nothing to stop the "flesh trade." Louis Fazio was active in the business, as was Dominic Picciurro, attorney Mike Megna, and to some degree Waukesha County sheriff Michael Lombardi. In Milwaukee, hotels and places such as the Tender Trap on Center Street were utilized. Appleton had the Blazing Stump, Sheboygan and Plymouth had their own places, and so did Green Bay. In the far north, Hurley was overflowing with sex and drugs; however, the source of the girls was invariably Milwaukee.

Milwaukee had a vice squad with Capt. Harry Kuszewski front and center as the spokesman. Yet, money often trumps the law, and with Kuszewski this was no exception. He was forced to resign after it was discovered he took bribes of cash and alcohol from the local madams. A greased palm here and there, and prostitution was virtually legal.

By the 1970s, the business of prostitution was changing. While it had not died—prostitution is the world's oldest profession and cannot be snuffed out—it did shift out of the control of the mafia. African American gangs took over the old stomping grounds and did not mix well with the Italians. (Whether it was due to racism or tradition is unknown, but the Milwaukee mafia very rarely interacted with African American gangs and never engaged in any business dealings with them.)

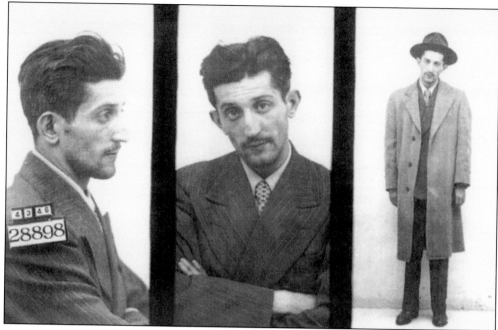

Cono Librizzi had a long record of burglaries and other crimes in Milwaukee. He was known to authorities as early as August 1935, when he acted as a pimp for 14-year-old Lillian Zamorski. In one day, she took part in more than a dozen sexual acts under the Holton Street Bridge. (Wisconsin Historical Society.)

On January 6, 1944, Eugene Reickman was hit with a blackjack and robbed of his car keys, wristwatch, and $170 by mob members. Police were quickly on the scene and caught John Angelo Mandello, George P. Leone, Pasquale Rosetti, August Pintaro, Lawrence Quartana, Anthony Scaffidi, and Joseph Guarniere. (Milwaukee Police Department.)

Here, an officer poses in front of Robert Barlow's basement on Kilbourn Avenue. Lawrence Quartana, then 34 years old, hid here after police arrived on the scene, but his efforts were in vain. (Milwaukee Police Department.)

Two officers point to a blood trail left by Anthony Scaffidi, who was shot by patrolman Charles Jackelin as he fled the scene. Scaffidi ran approximately 75 yards before his body gave out, and he died in the snow. (Milwaukee Police Department.)

Before finally collapsing, Anthony Scaffidi made his way to this garage and continued on. While the footprints in the snow may have stopped, the bloody palm prints were a dead giveaway of Scaffidi's location. (Milwaukee Police Department.)

This building on Water Street once held the Garden Tavern. Cesar Cortese went outside in September 1936 to investigate a car horn and was wounded in the scalp by a volley of shotgun slugs from unknown assailants. Cortese fired back with a pistol. Shortly thereafter, the tavern, which had 40 violations against it, lost its liquor license. (Author's collection.)

Nick Fucarino and his wife, Rose, operated a tavern at this location on Water Street. While they were under the radar for a while, police started taking notice after bartender Anthony Sciano was caught serving underage patrons in April 1942. (Author's collection.)

On February 17, 1926, Albert Speciale was shot in front of this grocery store on the corner of Jackson and Lyon Streets. On his person were letters from Antonio and Augustino Morici, two wholesale grocers from Chicago who had been murdered three weeks prior. (Milwaukee Police Department.)

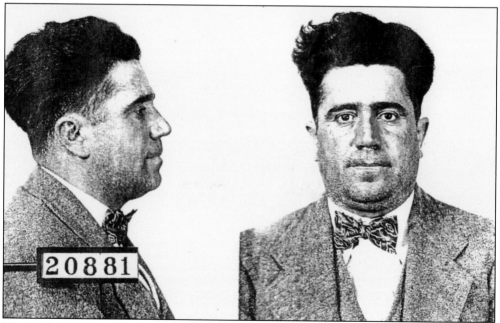

Vito Aiello, brother of Frank Aiello, came under suspicion in Frank's murder when police began uncovering his bootlegging connections. While Vito was never actively a suspect, the authorities had every reason to believe the booze and blood were connected. (Milwaukee Police Department.)

The Ogden Social Club was a floating gambling venture on Jackson Street. Pictured here is one of the locations where underworld figures hosted craps games and horse-race betting. Once one location was raided, the club moved to another building. There were at least nine raids. (Author's collection.)

Pictured again is Angelo LaMantia, now after an arrest in Pennsylvania. The court released him from charges of killing racketeer Morris Curran in 1931 after four principal witnesses, who were schoolgirls at the time, could not identify LaMantia as the man they saw that day. (Milwaukee Police Department.)

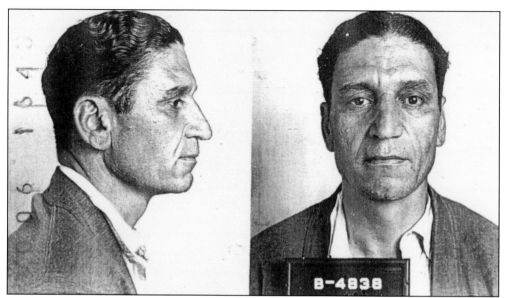

Tony Greco, an associate of Angelo LaMantia's in Waukegan, Illinois, was involved in a variety of petty gambling activities. Even smaller gambling activities such as numbers rackets could result in big payoffs for the mob if they played their cards right. (Milwaukee Police Department.)

This tavern on Bishop Avenue (now Wentworth Avenue), a meeting place for the Italian anarchists who bombed the central Milwaukee police station in 1917, was later owned by August Chiaverotti, the father of a top Milwaukee and Chicago mob associate. (Robert Tanzilo.)

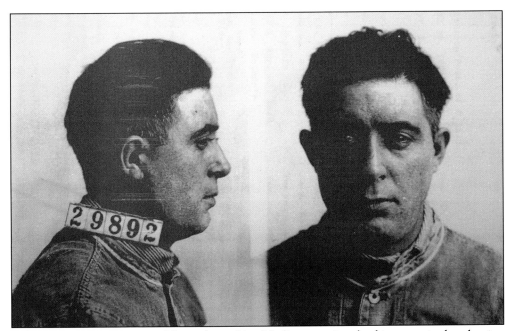

Jack Troia, a prominent part of the underworld in Madison, was involved in extensive bootlegging operations. The Troia name comes up again and again during the Prohibition years of Madison and Rockford, where Jack's brother Carlo lived. Another Troia, Vincenzo, spent his retirement years in Madison tending his garden while the FBI conducted weekly spot checks. (National Archives at Kansas City, Missouri.)

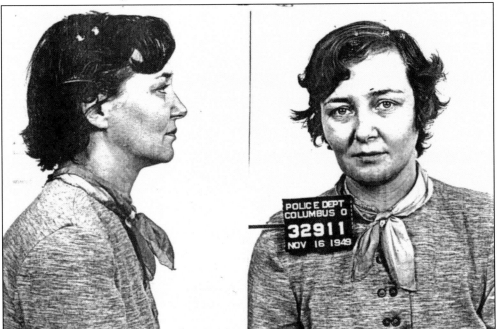

Violet Becker was one of John DiTrapani's many mistresses. While DiTrapani had a wife, he was openly known to date many other women, both single and married. Becker was married and actually involved in questionable liquor practices. (Milwaukee Police Department.)

Cono "the Weasel" Librizzi was one of the first hoodlums to move from Milwaukee's Third Ward into the Brady Street neighborhood. He lived in this house on Brady Street in August 1945 when he burglarized the Dutchland Dairy Store. Foolishly, he climbed in through a window while FBI agents were conducting surveillance on the store. (Author's collection.)

Michael Paul Enea, a suspect in the John DiTrapani murder, had a lengthy record going back to 1931 when he stole cars as a juvenile. He was a burglar and armed robber before finally getting picked up by Lt. Joseph Schalla of the Milwaukee Police Department for murder. (Milwaukee Police Department.)

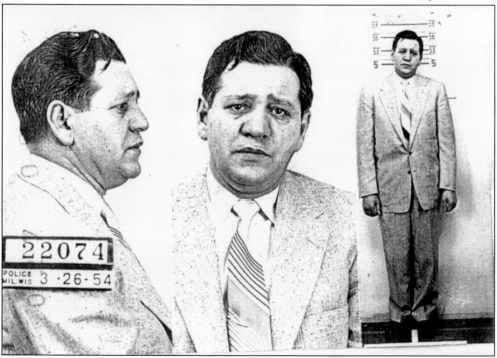

John DiTrapani was not only a well-to-do bar owner, but he also had strong ties to powerful members of the Milwaukee crime family. Former boss Sam Ferrara was his uncle and godfather, and Frank Balistrieri was a relative through marriage. (Milwaukee Police Department.)

F. Ryan Duffy, a former Democratic senator, went on to become a federal judge in the 1940s. Duffy presided over many mob trials during the following years. His first taste of the mafia was a June 1947 appearance by Steve John DeSalvo, who had been passing counterfeit sugar stamps. (Milwaukee County Historical Society.)

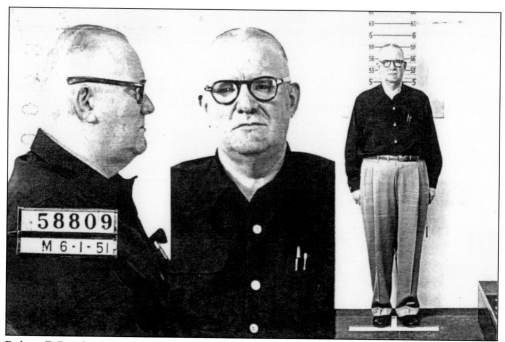

Robert F. Bundy was a suspect in the John DiTrapani murder. Bundy was a businessman who owned barbecue restaurants in Cleveland and St. Louis and co-owned one in Milwaukee with Felix and Molly Alderisio. (Milwaukee Police Department.)

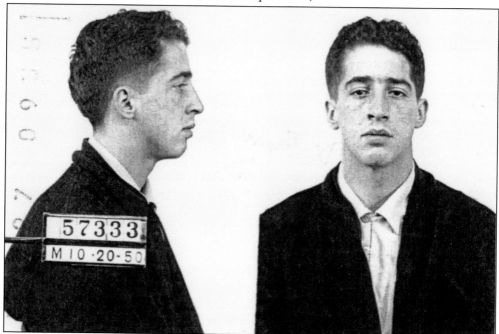

Salvatore Farina Jr. (pictured) was a convicted burglar, purse-snatcher, and batterer who was sent to prison for "indecent liberties" with a minor. The Farina family tree had more than a few bad apples. Salvatore's brother Mike Farina was ultimately murdered in Racine. (Milwaukee Police Department.)

SALLE HOTEL   729 N. Eleventh St. at W. Wisconsin Ave. -Milwaukee, Wiscons

When hiding out in Milwaukee, Blackie Sullivan and his wife, Edith (Johnson) Sullivan, stayed at the LaSalle Hotel. Officially, Blackie was not allowed within Milwaukee city limits by court order, but he turned up many more times before his death. (Milwaukee County Historical Society.)

Blackie and Edith Sullivan later rented this house on Layton Boulevard. While Blackie was away, the house was raided by police and found to contain dynamite and forged prescriptions for various drugs, including Demerol. Edith was arrested for the forgeries. (Author's collection.)

The Guardalabene & Amato Funeral Home was the primary business of its type used by members of the mafia, their families, and close associates. While staying in the Guardalabene family for generations, the business was eventually bought out by Schmidt & Bartelt. The funeral home no longer employs any Guardalabene family members. (Milwaukee County Historical Society.)

Salvatore "Sam" Ferrara was an old-timer in the Milwaukee crime family, having arrived from Rock Island in 1914. He served briefly as boss and later became the leader of the faction that opposed Frank Balistrieri as a boss. Due to a lack of support from Balistrieri's backers, Ferrara did not succeed. (Milwaukee County Historical Society.)

John Medrow was the chief of police for the Milwaukee suburb of Cudahy. He personally investigated the murder of James Scaffidi for six months but never solved it. Scaffidi was caught off-guard on December 12, 1919, and killed with his .38mm revolver still in his pocket. (Cudahy Public Library.)

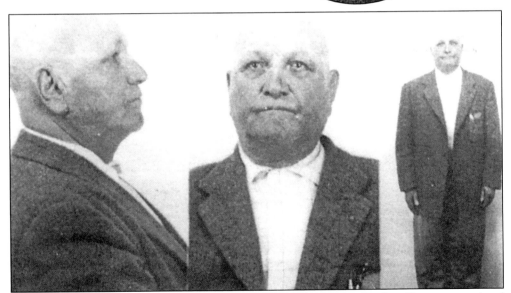

John Alioto took over as boss of the Milwaukee crime family in 1952 after Sam Ferrara was ordered to step down by the Chicago Outfit. Alioto was possibly Milwaukee's longest-serving member, with ties to every boss from 1920 through the 1990s. (Federal Bureau of Investigation.)

The Holiday House restaurant was burglarized by Walter Brocca and Jerome DiMaggio, with the men stealing a safe containing between $12,000 and $15,000. They were working on behalf of August Maniaci, who owed the Chicago Outfit $25,000 for a truckload of stolen meat. (Milwaukee County Historical Society.)

John DiTrapani was a former bootlegger and mob member with crime-family ties going back decades. He was considered a suspect in multiple homicides and other crimes. His death opened the floodgates of information to the police about the illicit liquor business. (Milwaukee Police Department.)

This restaurant on Farwell Avenue was once Chico's Bar-B-Q, owned by powerful mobster Frank LaGalbo. It was the last place John DiTrapani was seen in March 1954 before turning up dead. LaGalbo, Blackie Sullivan, and almost every mobster in town were considered suspects. (Author's collection.)

Mike Caruso had a history of petty crimes behind him, and it was another petty crime that sent him to Waupun Correctional Institution. Shortly after his brother Pasquale was murdered by the mafia, Caruso began carrying a gun for protection, and his lack of a permit landed him in prison. (Wisconsin Historical Society.)

Isadore "Charles" Crupi, the brother of vice lord Vince Crupi, was just as connected to the mob as his deported brother. Isadore was put in prison following a robbery in Sheboygan. With him were Lawrence Quartana, Pasquale Rosetti, and Frank Bruno. (Wisconsin Historical Society.)

Four

THE RISE OF FRANK BALISTRIERI

From the 1920s through the 1950s, many bosses had control of Milwaukee: Vito Guardalabene, Peter Guardalabene, Joseph Amato, Joseph Vallone, Sam Ferrara, and finally John Alioto. These were powerful and distinguished men—but also men of relatively low profile. They preferred to not see their names printed in the local press.

Frank Balistrieri was a different sort of boss. He rose to power on a wave of publicity. While not the head of the Milwaukee crime family until 1962, he was already seen as a leader by the police and newspapers as early as 1955. Balistrieri, with the help of his brother Peter and father, Joseph, took control of several taverns and nightclubs. City ordinances prevented one man from owning more than two taverns, but this problem was easily solved just by having someone else sign the paperwork.

Balistrieri was favored to become boss by Felix "Milwaukee Phil" Alderisio, who was the Chicago Outfit's big man in the city. If one wanted to win over Chicago, he had to go through Alderisio, and Balistrieri did just that. Frank's star also shone brightly by marrying Nina Alioto, the daughter of the reigning boss. Whether it was Alioto or Alderisio that ultimately granted Balistrieri the job is a matter of debate and something not even family members agree on.

While the decision to put Balistrieri on the throne was likely the beginning of the end for Milwaukee's mafia, it did have its perks. Balistrieri was ambitious and had a loyal crew of thugs and hangers-on. No other boss had the entourage Balistrieri had, lingering on his every word while sitting in coffee shops until the early hours of the night. Balistrieri was also related to Kansas City boss "Big Jim" Balistrere, who was more than happy to send some reinforcements to the "Cream City," including hard-nosed monsters Buster Balistrere and Joseph Gurera.

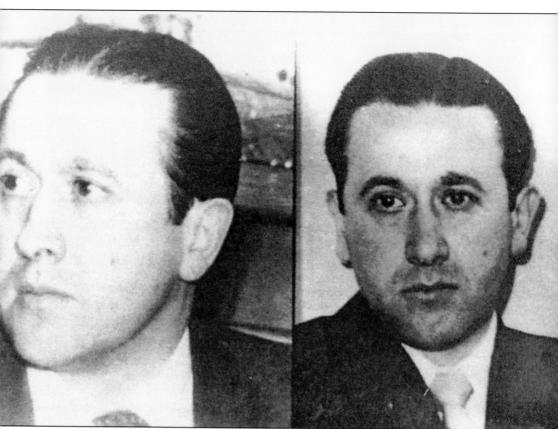

Frank Balistrieri, pictured here in FBI photographs, was the son-in-law of John Alioto. The attorney for John DiTrapani's estate, Fred R. Wright, suggested that Balistrieri take over DiTrapani's bar, Johnny's Round Up. While this was rejected by the city, it was the beginning of Balistrieri's takeover of Milwaukee taverns. (Federal Bureau of Investigation.)

James Gumina, pictured here, entered a tavern with Tony Gennaro and Peter Sorce and began smashing four slot machines. When arrested, Gumina protested that his actions should not have been a crime because slot machines were illegal anyway. (Wisconsin Historical Society.)

This postcard shows an early view of the city, facing west from Lake Michigan. The Italians of Milwaukee settled just south of here and later moved just north. They never strayed far from the heart of downtown. (Author's collection.)

Fazio's restaurant on Jackson Street was a popular hangout for mob members. In 1955, the restaurant was bombed, shattering windows in nearby homes. No one was caught, but suspicions fell on boxing promoter and union boss Phil Valley. (Author's collection.)

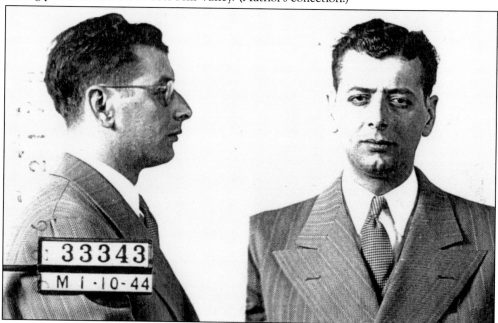

33343
M I·10-44

Anthony LaRosa was a known hoodlum who engaged in burglary and robbery. His most daring heist was probably when he hijacked a semitrailer, filled it with stolen meat, and then transported the meat to St. Louis in 1954. Crossing multiple state lines, he piqued the interest of the FBI. (Milwaukee Police Department.)

Carol Burns was a 22-year-old waitress at the Republican Hotel. On the evening of July 2, 1947, she was involved in a drunken argument with her fiancé, Louis Joseph Picciurro, over the course of several hours. The fight ended tragically, with Burns being fatally shot in the hip and shoulder by a .32mm pistol. (Milwaukee Police Department.)

After murdering his fiancé, Louis Joseph Picciurro threw the gun into a sewer drain at the corner of Pleasant and Jackson Streets. When questioned by Det. John Niederkorn the next day, Picciurro claimed to not remember killing Burns at all, blaming his actions on being drunk. When they were able to test it, his blood alcohol content was 0.15. (Milwaukee Police Department.)

A detective stands outside of Earl Steinhart's Club 3, the scene of the murder. Steinhart and Louis Behrend were able to offer their eyewitness testimony to police after Picciurro's memory mysteriously vanished. (Milwaukee Police Department.)

Seen here is another angle of the front of the tavern, showing the neighboring store offering costume jewelry for sale. Both businesses were on the 900 block of North Third Street and were torn down to make way for more modern establishments in the heart of downtown. (Milwaukee Police Department.)

This is the rear of Club 3. Unlike the front, the back of the tavern really illustrates how poor the neighborhood was, with buildings thrown together in a rather slapdash fashion. Beer enthusiasts will note the "Champagne of Bottled Beer" sign, evoking memories of when Miller called Milwaukee home. (Milwaukee Police Department.)

Louis Picciurro's car was taken in for the gathering of any evidence that could be found, such as bloodstains or powder marks. Nothing of value was retrieved, but enough witnesses were interviewed from various taverns (including Club 3 and Oscar Ruesch's Bungalow Tavern) that this was an open-and-shut case. Picciurro was convicted of first-degree murder and sentenced to life in Waupun Correctional Institution. (Milwaukee Police Department.)

Dominic Frinzi was the mafia's attorney and a prominent politician. This publicity photograph was taken when Frinzi was running for governor in the 1960s. It is perhaps lucky he lost since the stories of his mob connections are endless. (Milwaukee County Historical Society.)

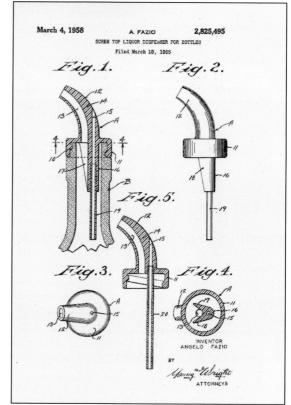

Angelo Fazio patented this device for pouring alcohol from bottles, which is still used today. One of his investors was none other than Ralph "Bottles" Capone, the brother of the more infamous "Scarface" Al Capone. (US Patent Office.)

This early-1950s image further shows the closeness of those in the mob. The men pictured here include Dr. Vito Guardalabene (back row, far right), Salvatore Ferrara (front row, far left), Pasquale Migliaccio (back row, far left), and Dr. Joseph E. Vaccaro, (next to Vaccaro), Migliaccio's son-in-law. The men are celebrating Rocky Graziano's (front row, third from the left) boxing victory with dinner at Chico's Bar-B-Q. (Milwaukee County Historical Society.)

Shown here in the 1940s are the three Cefalu brothers. Sam (right) became an associate of the mob, lying in order to provide an alibi for Louis Fazio, who had just murdered Mike Farina. The lie was useless, and Fazio was sent to prison. (Milwaukee County Historical Society.)

Det. Herman Bergin, along with Det. Walter English, was a lead investigator of the Pasquale Caruso mob murder in 1934. The killers were never caught. Bergin was known to the public since 1917, when he was caught in the blast that destroyed the central Milwaukee police station. (Robert Tanzilo.)

This marker shows where Our Lady of Pompeii Catholic Church once stood. Its destruction was also symbolic; as the Third Ward was being demolished, so too was the tight Italian community. More and more second-generation Italians moved to the suburbs. (Author's collection.)

Anthony "the Sheriff" Cefalu's gambling operation on Pierce Street, seen here, was raided in 1962. During the raid, the police arrested numerous mafia members and associates, including Steve DeSalvo, Joseph Gurera, Anthony Cefalu, Joseph Alioto, and Richard Milcarek. (Author's collection.)

Nichelle Nichols, best known as Uhura on *Star Trek*, started out her career as a dancer in one of Frank Balistrieri's nightclubs. In her autobiography, she tells the story of how Balistrieri's attorney, Dominic Frinzi, tried to seduce her with furs and other gifts.

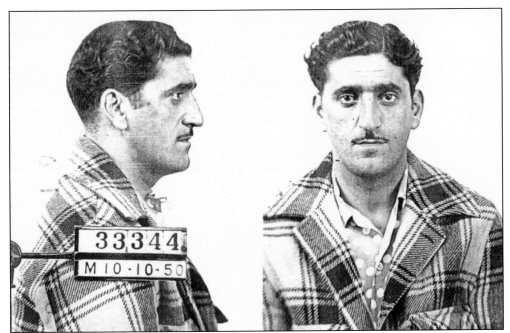

Joseph Charles Guarniere was a noted safecracker and partner with Anthony LaRosa. His arrest record is lengthy, starting in his teens and going well into the 1950s. It was common practice for police to show photographs of Guarniere to crime witnesses, as he was a perennial suspect. (Milwaukee Police Department.)

John Hadukovich was a Minnesota transplant who was quickly caught by the Secret Service for counterfeiting. Coins he produced were still found in circulation years after his capture. (National Archives at Kansas City, Missouri.)

This house on Warren Avenue was owned by Joseph Latona, who served a variety of functions for the Milwaukee mob. One of his biggest moments of infamy came when he was arrested for running a brothel. (Author's collection.)

Louis Greco (left), shown here with Frank Cosentino, was a hoodlum from Kenosha. He was married to William Covelli's stepdaughter and, in later years, had a falling out with Milwaukee mobster Dominic Principe, an associate of Covelli's son Jeff. (Author's collection.)

This is the actual gun owned by Louis Paradise, today in the possession of his grandson. Paradise's role in the mob is unclear: was he merely a victim or something more? His association with out-of-state hoodlums suggests the latter. He apparently was selling supplies to Cleveland, Ohio, bootleggers, who shorted him $3,000. (Author's collection.)

Tony Accardo (right), the boss of the Chicago Outfit, was the real power behind the Milwaukee mafia. While the Milwaukee crime family was largely independent, Accardo was consulted for important decisions and later heard arguments from old-timers about Balistrieri's poor leadership. (Federal Bureau of Investigation.)

When hoodlum Jack Enea was murdered in Waukesha, one of the theories circulating was that he had burglarized Joseph Sciortino's Bakery on Van Buren Street and his death was ordered by John Alioto. The crime was especially grievous because Sciortino was Enea's uncle. (Milwaukee County Historical Society.)

Joseph Alioto, bartender Joseph Lorenzo, and waiter Mariano Rugeri were arrested at the Jefferson Inn on January 26, 1930. Dry agents destroyed 92 pints of gin, 18 pints of whiskey, a gallon of grain alcohol, and seven 50-gallon barrels of beer. This was just one of countless raids. (Milwaukee County Historical Society.)

Ralph Capone, although based out of Hurley, Wisconsin, made monthly trips to Milwaukee to meet up with Angelo Fazio and Joseph Gagliano in the late 1950s. Federal agents tracked his every move and believed he might have been trafficking in dope he stored at the Milwaukee airport. (Federal Bureau of Investigation.)

This home on Fourteenth Street was once the residence of one-armed thug Max Adonnis. Max's given name was Gajewski, but he changed it to sound more Italian to fit in with the gangsters he admired. He was a lackey for the rest of his life. (Author's collection.)

Fifty-ninth Street is where one can find the former residence of jewel thief Frank Stelloh. Because he was not Italian, Stelloh could not ever officially become a mafia member; however, he was seen as Frank Balistrieri's right-hand man and as high ranking as any "made man." (Author's collection.)

One of the two hotels that Ralph Capone frequented was the Ambassador. He also visited Frenchy's Restaurant and attended Milwaukee Braves games while in town. The FBI's constant trailing of Capone led him to complain to the police on July 2, 1958. (Author's collection.)

Jack Enea lived in this Jackson Street house. While Enea was never a very important part of the Milwaukee crime family, he showed up from time to time as a partner in various arrests. A long criminal record, however, is only evidence of being good at getting caught, not at being a thief. (Author's collection.)

Walter Brocca lived at this home on Van Buren Street. Brocca amounted to little more than a patsy for Frank Balistrieri, doing grunt work and poor-quality construction projects. He was a candidate to be made but was strung along for several months and may never have had the honor. (Author's collection.)

John Alioto's son Angelo became a founder of the National Italian Invitational Golf Tournament for Charities, believed to be the oldest ethnic golf tournament in the United States. While it was a legitimate enterprise, due to the Alioto family's connections known hoodlums also attended the event. (Author's collection.)

James Jennaro lived in this apartment complex on Prospect Avenue. He started as an employee of Frank Balistrieri, but he later worked as a thug for Sally Papia, the owner of Sally's Steak House. Balistrieri was not thrilled and threatened to, from a recorded wiretap, "drop" Jennaro and his business partner Frank Trovato. (Author's collection.)

Pitch's Lounge and Restaurant on Humboldt Avenue has a long history of mob ties, with several members of the Picciurro family engaging in illegal gambling operations. Frank Balistrieri's mother was also a Picciurro. Today, the family has no ties and is strictly legitimate (and makes a very fine cocktail). (Author's collection.)

When John Alioto retired from Milwaukee's Sanitation Department, he focused his time and energy on the Alioto Market, operated out of this building on North Booth Street. He was assisted in the day-to-day operations by his wife, Catherine. (Author's collection.)

Russell Enea owned this home in the Milwaukee suburbs. He was involved in various routine mob functions and followed in the footsteps of family members Jack Enea and Joseph Enea, a partner in Joe's Spaghetti House with Walter Brocca. (Author's collection.)

Photographer Clarence Leino was often first on the scene and kept mob members on their toes, even when the police did not. This Leino photograph captures a group of men in a natural moment, without posing or trying to show off a persona. (Sandy Leino [photographer's daughter].)

In 1961, when the "heat" at Sammy's 808 Club got too hot, Sam Cefalu moved his gambling operation into his home on Holton Street. While it kept the heat down a little bit because police could not enter the building without a warrant, it was no secret where the money and wagering information was kept. (Author's collection.)

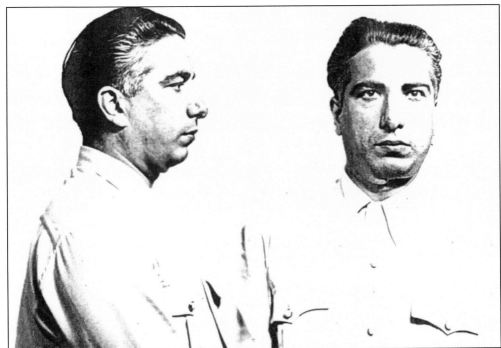

This mug shot is an example of excellent police work hampered by inadequate record keeping. The photograph was found in the DiTrapani murder file, but without a booking number his name has been lost; the image may even have been misfiled. (Milwaukee Police Department.)

This was the Jackson Street residence of John Picciurro, a notorious fence. Such burglars as William Giacalone, John Prediger, and Dominic Vitrano burglarized businesses around Milwaukee, and the goods were sold through Picciurro and Nick Fucarino. (Author's collection.)

Serving as a dormitory for Marquette University today, the Stratford-Arms Hotel on Wisconsin Avenue was another hotel used by Ralph Capone during business trips under the pseudonym R. C. James. His room number was 218. (Milwaukee County Historical Society.)

Jerome Mandella testified that on the night of the shooting of Mike Farina, he was visiting his sister Mrs. Thomas Tarantino at her tavern, the Highway Tap, which was in this VanBuren Street building. Mandella was sentenced to prison for his part in the slaying. (Author's collection.)

The Shorecrest Hotel was owned and operated by Balistrieri brothers Joseph and John. Their father, mob boss Frank Balistrieri, ran his business from a booth in the hotel's restaurant, Snug's. It is said he had a red phone for his business calls. (Author's collection.)

Louis Manna (right) operated a grocery store with Frank Cosentino. While it is hard to definitively say that Manna was a criminal, he did associate with the Cosentino and Covelli families and was present at the murder of Frank Paparas in 1928 according to newspaper reports and the coroner's hearing. (Author's collection.)

Anthony DePalma lived in this Booth Street home. DePalma, a bartender for John DiTrapani, was robbed in broad daylight of $9,000 and then forced inside of a car and dropped off at the corner of Twenty-fifth and Vine Streets. He told police he did not see the men who abducted him. (Author's collection.)

Herb Kohl, a Democratic senator and owner of the Milwaukee Bucks, was once a friend of Sally Papia, and it was not unusual to see him inside her restaurant, Sally's Steak House. On one occasion, she gave him advice on opening his own business (which he never did).

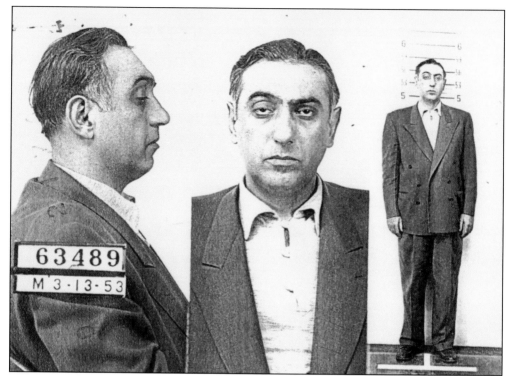

Sam Vermiglio was the most colorful gangster in Milwaukee. A suspect in multiple murders, robberies, counterfeiting, hijackings, and more, he was wanted by multiple state and federal agencies. Even after being deported twice, he continued his notorious career. (Milwaukee Police Department.)

This house on White Rock Avenue in Waukesha was the scene of a shoot-out between Pasquale Caruso and the wife of his bootlegging partner, Pasquale "Patsy" Schirripa. White Rock Avenue was the center of the Italian underworld in Waukesha and housed an illicit brewery. (Author's collection.)

Five

THE MAD BOMBER'S REIGN

Frank Balistrieri had many nicknames, including "Frankie Bal" and "Mr. Big," but the most colorful moniker he was given was the "Mad Bomber"—a name he earned.

Balistrieri's reign spread Milwaukee control over Racine and Kenosha, which had traditionally been run by the Camorra (basically, the Neapolitan version of the mafia). He briefly tried but failed to take Madison. The mob had stakes in more taverns and ran more gambling operations (even getting a cut from poker games), and most notoriously it tried to gain a monopoly over jukeboxes and other coin-operated devices.

Herman Paster ran jukeboxes and slot machines in St. Paul and Milwaukee. One evening, after arriving home in St. Paul from Milwaukee, he was shot dead, and soon his routes were controlled by the mob. Tony Biernat had a small route in Kenosha and on the military base near Waukegan. When he refused to sell his business to the Milwaukee crime family, he was found buried in a shallow grave. Balistrieri also tried to scam people into buying used machines as new that were merely old machines with new faces. To say he pushed people into buying is an understatement.

As for the Mad Bomber nickname, more than a couple of men understood this moniker. "Lefty" Rosenthal in Las Vegas had his car blown up and barely made it out alive (fictionalized in the film *Casino*). Vincent Maniaci found sticks of dynamite under his hood and was forced to flee to Hawaii. Reporter Ned Day had his car blown up (luckily he was not inside at the time). At least one man, August Palmisano, was actually killed in a blast. The bombs of Milwaukee may not have rivaled Cleveland, but they were more than enough to ruffle the feathers of would-be stool pigeons.

This home on Shepard Avenue, now a historic landmark known as the Edward H. Inbusch house, was purchased by Frank Balistrieri in 1960, and he lived there until his death in 1993. When the family had an estate sale, Milwaukee citizens waited hours just to get a peek inside. (Author's collection.)

The Safety Building is Milwaukee's home for the police and fire departments, along with some courtrooms. While the police today have multiple buildings, once not too long ago suspected criminals spent more time than they wished behind these walls getting grilled by detectives. (Author's collection.)

Brothers William and Jeff Covelli, shown here as kids being sent to Italy for school, both grew up to be hoodlums. Jeff ended up committing armed robbery in Racine, and William (known as "Wheezer") rose even higher in the ranks. At one point, he was kidnapped and dangled by his belt over a shallow grave. (Author's collection.)

No boss before Frank Balistrieri was as powerful, and none had such attention paid to him by the media and police. His selection as chief was warned against by those who wished to avoid the authorities coming down on the family, and those warnings turned out to be very prescient. (Milwaukee County Historical Society.)

It is unknown what is being celebrated in this image, but the men identified are Frank Bonfiglio (1), Pasquale Migliaccio (2), Sam Ferrara (3), Santo Marino (4), and John DiTrapani (5). (John Anderson.)

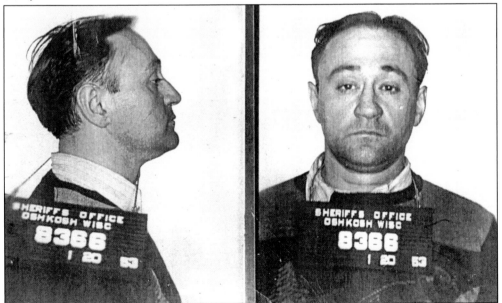

David Ferdinand had a police record that covered over 20 years. He had been arrested for robbery, burglary, impersonating an officer, assault, obtaining money under false pretenses, and battery. In 1954, he was wanted as a suspect in the John DiTrapani slaying. (Milwaukee Police Department.)

Gov. John Reynolds was scorned by the FBI after he told the press that the feds were looking into the Biernat murder, ruining their secrecy; however, he also proved helpful, directing them to suspects like Laddie Henry Steinhoff, a Biernat competitor who formerly lived near the Richard Bong State Recreation Area.

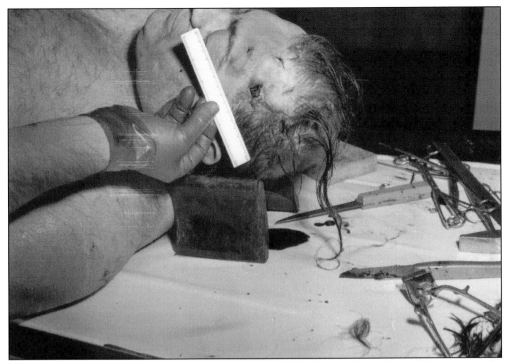

Isadore Pogrob was the victim of a mob hit despite not being a gangster himself. He operated a tavern and nightclub in Milwaukee known as the Brass Rail. Although the performances there could be considered racy, he was not known to be a criminal. (Mequon Police Department.)

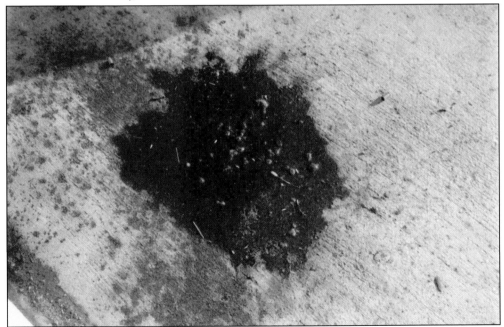

Although hard to discern in black and white, this was the stain left from the Pogrob slaying. Spent bullet casings are visible, and the Mequon Police Department notes state the pieces seen here are "gore," presumably brain matter. (Mequon Police Department.)

Pogrob was blindfolded and shot here at the edge of a road in rural Mequon, north of Milwaukee. His body was then dumped over the side. (Mequon Police Department.)

The body was found under this bridge. A skin diver spent the day searching for clues but was unable to come up with anything. The case is unsolved to this day. (Mequon Police Department.)

This dummy was left to taunt the Mequon Police Department. It may be possible that the plump dummy represents Isadore Pogrob, who weighed in excess of 320 pounds at his death. (Mequon Police Department.)

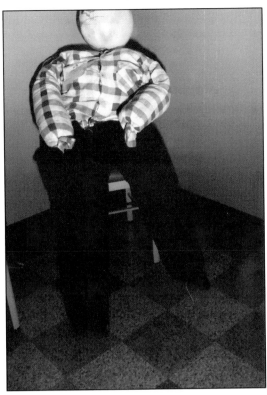

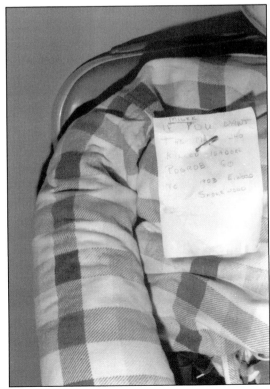

A close-up of the dummy reveals a note offering a suggestion to Mequon police chief Robert Milke. The address listed did not advance the case, and it now sits cold, forever a mystery. (Mequon Police Department.)

A small bomb detonated in the Peter Sciortino Bakery in 1962. Special agents Richard Thompson and Alexander LeGrand questioned Sciortino the following year, asking him about rumors that he was paying $30 per week for protection. The rumors were denied. (Author's collection.)

Alioto's in Wauwatosa is not only a great restaurant but was once also a classy meeting place for gangsters. After the wedding of Peter Balistrieri's daughter, hoodlums from Milwaukee, Kenosha, Kansas City, and elsewhere held a reception at the restaurant. Many more mob events were held here. Still in business today after more than 50 years, it was later taken over by John's son Angelo. (Author's collection.)

This building on Downer Avenue once housed Mr. Tony's, a tavern and restaurant operated by hoodlum Salvatore Seidita. Following the funeral of Madison mob boss Benny DiSalvo in 1964, several mobsters met in the basement to complain about FBI surveillance at the funeral. (Author's collection.)

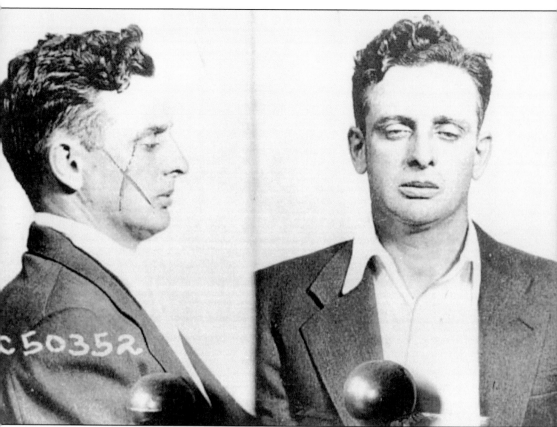

Although Chicago mobster Roger Touhy (pictured) had been dead five years, the FBI overheard Milwaukee member Walter Brocca talking about him in 1964. Part of the conversation included the ambiguous phrase, "Too many big people were involved, and now he is dead." (Federal Bureau of Investigation.)

Pasquale Scalici (center), also known as Frank Little, was a little person and former circus clown. He was related through marriage to the men who ran the Ogden Social Club, and by the 1960s he was bookmaking on behalf of Walter Brocca. (Michael Scalici.)

Scalici (left) made many friends and acquaintances over the years. He is shown here in his younger days alongside Babe Ruth. One suspects that Scalici was not drawn naturally to crime but was too well connected to avoid the profits of running a numbers racket. (Michael Scalici.)

This building on Pleasant Street
served as an office for mob men
Carl Dentice and Joseph Spero,
who were listed as licensed to
operate amusement devices by
the City of Milwaukee. In reality,
while they had the licenses, both
men were fronting for Frank
Balistrieri. (Author's collection.)

Joseph Balistrieri, son of Frank
Balistrieri, earned a law degree
from the University of Wisconsin-
Madison in 1965. His brother John
also earned a law degree, but Joseph
was by far the more successful and
publicly known of the two. His
graduation party featured 500 guests,
many of them out-of-state hoodlums.
(University of Madison Law Library.)

The December 1965 wedding of Rose Fucarino and Anthony Schiavo, who are pictured here in later years, was a grand event for the mafia. Both had a father in the Milwaukee and Madison families, respectively, and this union brought 1,000 guests from Milwaukee, Madison, Rockford, and elsewhere. The attendants included Balistrieri relatives and the daughter of Racine bootlegger Jack Iannello. (Dan Curd.)

Steve DeSalvo, Frank Balistrieri's second in command, lived in this house on 82nd Street. Besides the constant FBI surveillance, DeSalvo endured a month of 24-hour "bumper lock" surveillance from the police, too. His every move, meal, and conversation was photographed and recorded. (Author's collection.)

This mansion on Washington Boulevard belonged to Julius and Martha Theilacker. They were the unlucky victims of Anthony Pipito and Salvatore DiMaggio, who had decided to commit a daytime robbery and attempted to do so after tying the elderly couple up. Both robbers were quickly apprehended though, thanks to the watchful eyes of neighbor William Swan. (Author's collection.)

On August 4, 1968, there was a stag dinner honoring the son of an unidentified La Cosa Nostra member who was getting married. Nick Fucarino, Walter Brocca, Joseph Spero, and other hoodlums were in attendance. The dinner was held at Vitucci's, located on East North Avenue. (Author's collection.)

Frank Balistrieri was at Sally's Steak House inside the Knickerbocker Hotel until very late in the evening Christmas Eve 1968, causing his wife to get very upset. She called Sally Papia and told her to stay away from Balistrieri. Around this time, Sally was also plotting to overthrow Balistrieri's reign. (Author's collection.)

According to a 1969 *Life* magazine article, Mayor Joseph Alioto of San Francisco provided mafia leaders "with bank loans, legal services, business counsel and the protective mantle of his respectability. In return he has earned fees, profits, political support and campaign contributions." Alioto was closely related to the Milwaukee Aliotos.

Mayor Alioto, as board chairman for the First San Francisco Bank, personally arranged loans totaling $105,000 for mafia hit man Jimmy "the Weasel" Fratianno, pictured here; Alioto did not deny this claim. Fratianno later became the highest-ranking mafia member to become a known informant. (Federal Bureau of Investigation.)

Mob boss John Alioto (left) is seen here in the 1950s with another prominent Milwaukee businessman meeting the Italian ambassador (right). Alioto, besides his criminal history, was an important part of the legitimate Italian community. (Milwaukee Historical Society.)

Frank Balistrieri's father, Joseph, died of natural causes on March 3, 1971, and Frank's father-in-law John Alioto was nowhere to be found at the funeral. The two had been at odds for a while over Frank's treatment of the older members, as well as over allegations that Frank was cheating on his wife. (Author's collection.)

Frank Balistrieri was running a jukebox business out of this building on Downer Avenue. Unknown to him, the building had been set up for wiretaps, and federal agents were eavesdropping on his conversations. (Author's collection.)

After the eavesdropping was discovered, Frank Balistrieri sued the government with the help of his son, attorney Joseph Balistrieri. A chief witness during the trial was Santo Marino, who was now elderly and confined to his apartment on Prospect Avenue in the building pictured here. (Author's collection.)

This home, owned by Sally Papia, was burglarized in 1971, and jewelry valued at $49,000 was stolen. Some rings were discovered in the possession of Edwin S. Siegel, the operator of a barbershop on West North Avenue. Another ring was purchased for $700 by dentist Dr. Alvin Gloyeck. (Author's collection.)

85990
3-25-71

Max Adonnis, a thug who worked for Sally Papia, held Allen Quindt hostage in a West Side garage and threatened to kill him for the theft, which he was apparently not part of. Quindt had his jaw broken but escaped with his life. (Steve Spingola.)

Frank Balistrieri was approached by San Diego real estate developer Allen Glick (pictured here), a friend of his son Joseph, regarding Las Vegas. Glick wanted to build a casino in Las Vegas but lacked the funding. Money was then pulled from the Teamsters Central States Pension Fund. (Federal Bureau of Investigation.)

After the Teamsters' pension fund was raided to establish casinos for the mafia, Allen Glick paid a kickback of $600,000 to Teamsters president Frank Fitzsimmons, seen here, and Cleveland Teamsters leader William Presser. (Author's collection.)

HOTEL SCHROEDER • MILWAUKEE, WIS.

The coffee shop of the Hotel Schroeder was a hangout spot for mobster John DiTrapani and liquor salesman Meyer "Babe" Shaw. This hotel was also the preferred choice of jukebox racketeer Herman Paster while in town from St. Paul. Coincidentally, both Paster and DiTrapani were later murdered. (Author's collection.)

Leroy Bell, the owner of the Tender Trap (pictured here), sent girls to Sally's Steak House for the purposes of prostitution around 1973. For $100, the women engaged in various acts of sexual perversion. One prostitute, Katherine "Casey" Erbach, later joined a convent. (Author's collection.)

Mobster Vincent Maniaci was turned down for an operator's license for Little Caesar's (a tavern on Water Street that today is the Trocadero) in July 1975 due to his criminal record. Instead, Richard W. Czarnecki took over the business despite objections from Alderman Edward Griffin, who believed Czarnecki was a front man. (Author's collection.)

Kansas City's Nick Civella and Milwaukee's Frank Balistrieri fought over their share of the Las Vegas money. When they approached a higher authority for resolution, Chicago Outfit leader Joseph "Joey Doves" Aiuppa, seen here hiding his face, demanded that the Outfit receive a 25-percent tax as its cut in skimming operations. (Federal Bureau of Investigation.)

On September 11, 1975, gambling operator August Joseph Maniaci, a suspected informer, was murdered by five gunshots to the head, along with one to the left arm and one to the left shoulder, in an alley outside his Milwaukee home on North Newhall Street, pictured here. (Author's collection.)

Albert Tocco was suspected of ordering the hit on Maniaci. Chicago mobsters Charles Nicoletti and Nick D'Andrea were both accused of doing the job by those familiar with the situation. The two men were both killed within six years. (Federal Bureau of Investigation.)

Six

BALISTRIERI'S DOWNWARD SPIRAL

Frank Balistrieri may have been the man to most expand the power and influence of the Milwaukee crime family, but he was also a key component of its downfall.

Angelo G. Provinzano, president of Milwaukee's Dairy Lane shops, was considered for the position of next mafia boss over Balistrieri because the latter had too many run-ins with police and received an excessive amount of headlines in the newspapers. Provinzano, by contrast, had no arrest record and received only positive press. For whatever reason, Balistrieri became the new boss.

Balistrieri's arrogance was the end of the Milwaukee crime family. His reign was plagued by constant media attention, police surveillance, and an FBI that had grown more aware of the mafia's power since the Apalachin bust of 1957. When Frank went to prison for tax fraud, he put his brother Peter in charge of his affairs. A wiser move would have been to step down and reduce the heat. His move did quite the opposite, as Peter was already a wanted man.

Frank also had a tendency to ignore or distance himself from the old-timers (or "Mustache Petes"). This disrespect bred dissention and had more established members going over Balistrieri's head to Chicago with endless complaints. The family was small enough, and when it became factionalized, it had even weaker legs to stand on. At the time of Balistrieri's death in 1993, the old-timers had already faded away, and the younger generation grew up without a strong organization.

Whether the remaining family members associated with Chicago after this or disbanded is unclear, but the Milwaukee crime family had become extinct, completely ruined by the death of one man.

LANKINTON HOUSE -- MILWAUK

Plankinton Avenue, located just across the river from downtown, featured mobster John Triliegi's restaurant and the August Axt jewelry company, the scene of a $37,500 heist. The Plankinton House was the home of many offices, including that of mob attorney Abe Skolnick. (Author's collection.)

Frank LaGalbo lived in this home on Albion Street and was able to walk to Chico's Bar-B-Q through his backyard, which was helpful for evading the constant police surveillance. LaGalbo was later banished from the Milwaukee mob (joining up with Chicago Heights) and ultimately committed suicide. (Author's collection.)

Joseph Balistrieri made a name for himself defending his father's friends and associates. During one 1975 case, he implored the jury, "I don't know how you can convict him, based on the testimony of the gypsies, tramps, vagabonds and thieves that the government has presented in this case." His client was acquitted. (Milwaukee County Historical Society.)

POGROB

SON
ISADORE POGROB
DIED JAN. 6. 1960
AGE 37 YEARS
פנ יצחק בר מאיר
נפ ז' טבת תשכ
ת נ צ ב ה

Isadore Pogrob rests peacefully in this grave at Beth Hamedrosh Hagodel Cemetery; in the background is Miller Park. His tavern, the Brass Rail, was taken over by mobster Vito Aiello, the grandson and namesake of Milwaukee's original mob boss, Vito Guardalabene. (Milwaukee County Historical Society.)

After the murder of John DiTrapani, a check of his phone records revealed multiple calls to the Silver Frolics in Chicago, and police determined he had made occasional trips there. The Frolics was operated by high-ranking mobster Joseph Aiuppa and managed by fight-fixer Felix Bocchiccio. (Milwaukee County Historical Society.)

Milwaukee detective John Schroeder was forced to resign in late December 1975 after it was discovered that he was making visits to the home of Sally Papia (pictured). The purpose of these visits is unclear, but the conduct was viewed as unprofessional by Internal Affairs. (Author's collection.)

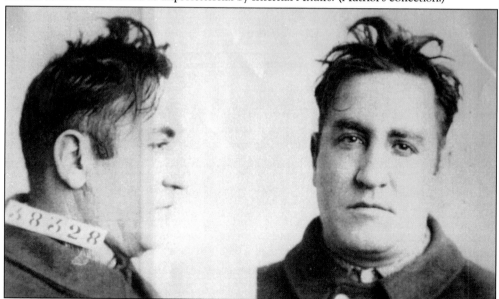

Anthony Musso was the mob boss of Rockford, Illinois, in the 1950s. The FBI stumbled upon him after checking John Alioto's phone records and seeing Musso's home turn up. Coincidentally, within months of their starting to look into Musso, he died of natural causes. What links these men shared may never be known. (National Archives at Kansas City, Missouri.)

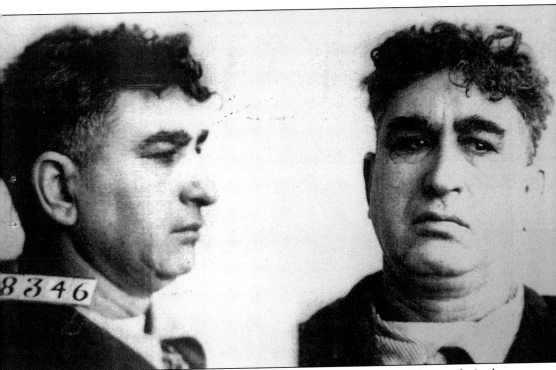

Peter SanFilippo was another Rockford hoodlum with ties to Wisconsin. Along with Anthony Musso, SanFilippo was involved in a bootlegging ring with Milwaukee mobster John Masina, who was based in Racine. Masina was murdered in August 1931, and his Rockford associates were shipped off Leavenworth Penitentiary. (National Archives at Kansas City, Missouri.)

Peter Frampton testified in Milwaukee at a John Doe hearing concerning drug trafficking by mob associate Charles Gottlieb. Frampton knew the Gottliebs because they were friends with Milwaukee native Penny McCall, Frampton's girlfriend at the time. When Frampton was performing in Milwaukee, the Gottliebs were backstage.

Frank Balistrieri's daughter Benedetta followed her second husband, Johnny Contardo, the former lead singer for the band Sha Na Na, to Hollywood in 1982. (Johnny Contardo.)

The October 4, 1982, car bombing of mob associate and Stardust Resort and Casino executive Frank "Lefty" Rosenthal (pictured) in Las Vegas was attributed to Frank Balistrieri. Rosenthal's Cadillac was in the parking lot of Tony Roma's, and he survived only because a metal plate was installed under the driver's seat. (Federal Bureau of Investigation.)

August Palmisano, suspected of being an informant, was also in a car that blew up after he started it in his underground parking garage, which is beneath this apartment building. Not only was Palmisano killed instantly, but also at least 20 other cars were damaged. (Author's collection.)

Ned Day was formerly a bartender for Frank Balistrieri but left Milwaukee for Las Vegas to become a reporter. While there, he broke numerous stories on the mob's influence over casinos. In 1986, the mafia showed Day how much they liked his reporting when they set his car ablaze. (George Knapp.)

On November 30, 1984, police searched the condo of Anthony Pipito and found 2,637 grams of cocaine, Milwaukee police badge no. 526, Milwaukee County Sheriff stationery, two pipe bombs, a disassembled shotgun, and two handguns. Pipito was also connected to the slaying of Anthony Biernat after his palm print was taken. (Author's collection.)

This house on Brady Street was the home of Max Adonnis. On the morning he was killed in 1989, Adonnis walked down the front steps and across the street to his restaurant, Giovanni's. After unlocking the door for the cleaning lady, he was overtaken by two gunmen and forced to his knees. Defenseless, he was shot in the back of the head and died. (Author's collection.)

This strip mall on Van Buren Street was the location of Giovanni's restaurant. Perhaps due to the murder there, it was torn down and replaced with new, less macabre surroundings. Another piece of Milwaukee history was washed away. (Author's collection.)

After being convicted for gambling, Salvatore Librizzi was hit with a heavy tax burden. Unable to pay, the government went after his home, pictured here, in Whitefish Bay. (Author's collection.)

When Frank Balistrieri died in 1993, the Milwaukee crime family died with him. While some speculation remains that there has been at least one boss since, no evidence has surfaced to confirm this. The Milwaukee crime family is now considered "defunct" or "extinct" by the FBI. (Author's collection.)

John Balistrieri, Frank's son, owned this home on Kenilworth Place. During the unusually cold winter of 1979, the pipes burst. John put in an insurance claim for $51,523 and gave the plumbing job to a friend of his. He was investigated and charged with insurance fraud for inflating the damage but was ultimately acquitted. (Author's collection.)

Just because the family has been dismantled, it does not mean all the secrets of their organization have been solved. Even almost 20 years after Balistrieri's passing, the FBI refuses to divulge the identity of the woman in this photograph with him. (Federal Bureau of Investigation.)

DISCOVER THOUSANDS OF LOCAL HISTORY BOOKS FEATURING MILLIONS OF VINTAGE IMAGES

Arcadia Publishing, the leading local history publisher in the United States, is committed to making history accessible and meaningful through publishing books that celebrate and preserve the heritage of America's people and places.

Find more books like this at
www.arcadiapublishing.com

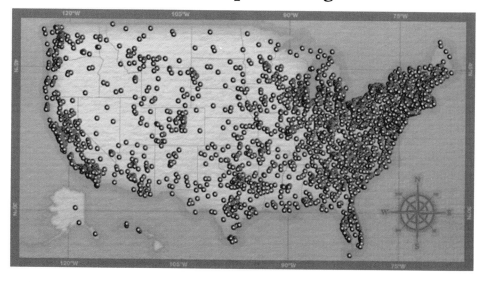

Search for your hometown history, your old stomping grounds, and even your favorite sports team.